Desolate Soul

2nd Edition

I0191122

Brian Stoaks

Desolate Soul

Poems by
Brian Stoaks

Table of Contents

From the Author   5

Setting Suns   6

Our Hearts   7

Over the Souls   8

Rivers of Gold   9

Strangest of Strangers   10

Want to Dream   11

No Longer Say   12

For the World to See   13

With All That I Was and I Am Now   14

When I Close My Eyes   15

Reflect   16

I am Not Afraid   17

Forgotten   18

I Only Smile When I'm Sleeping   19

Darkness   20

Desolate Soul   21

Finally Smile   22

With Salty Tears   23

Shall Always Be Love   25

From the Author

I was born in 1971 in Kansas City, Missouri. I have lived here all my life and have no intention of ever leaving this great city I call home. I am a father of 6 wonderful children.

Through the years I have had to deal with love, depression, divorce and various other struggles. Poetry has been one of my main coping skills. It helps me smile and keeps me from staying too down. Instead of getting angry, I write. When I write it allows my mind the freedom to fly away from the darkness and into the greatness of poetry. Writing poetry, for me, seems to be an easy way to explain my feelings or thoughts so they can be shared with others.

I'd like to dedicate "Desolate Soul" to several people. First, to my wonderful children, Ashley, Tyler, Zachary, Shareena, Samantha, and Brooke. Also to Lesley Roy of Ireland. I listen to the album Unbeautiful every time I write and it inspires me. I also dedicate this book to God. Without You I would have never made it this far. This is also for all of my fans who have been reading my work for quite some time and encouraging me to get this done. Finally, to my publishers Julie and David for believing in me and helping me through this journey of allowing my dream to come true.

I love you! God loves you! We should all love each other! Thank you!

Setting Suns

Living the days with cloudy eyes
Unable to clearly see the steps ahead
Standing in motion
Unable to move forward
The mind not as clear as crystal water streams

Thoughts speedily racing towards nowhere fast
Keeping my eyes open
Staring into the darkness
Heart thumping like the drums of a marching band
Echoing throughout the night causing my fears to deepen

Walking into the days ahead unable to see a path
Unconscionably screaming into the ears of strangers
Searching for the golden key to open the doors ahead
I fall only to crawl like infants
Towards the shining stars

Never denying my heart is sick with habits
Vigorous actions repeated daily to ease the pain inside
Crying from pain held within by the silence of my tongue
Unable to speak
I admit
If not only to myself
I am the habit of setting suns

Our Hearts

Whispering winds telling secrets beneath the oak tree
Guiding thoughts of happiness
Securing hope for tomorrow
Believing in eternal warmth
To cover the feeling of happiness
Secretly implanting thoughts of tomorrow
As we speak of destiny

Trickling water listened to
As it flows through the creek rocks
Never ending like the songs of birds
Heard in the morning sun
Laughter echoes between the canyon walls
As we speak of memories
Slowly we deepen our inner thoughts
Of our longing to know one another

White trails from jets crisscross the morning sky
Traveling people on a mission of purpose
To satisfy a need
We lay together staring into the blue world
Thanking God we're here
Flirting with thoughts of tomorrows to come
Arousing the senses of sweetness

The beginning is never the end
When laying together in secret
Forbidden mornings of lustful romance
While lying in the fields of peace
Rekindling the fire of younger years
When life was much too simple
Starting a journey of replenishing love
As our hearts melt into one

Over the Souls

Forgettable smiles tend to be suppressed into the mind
Some day while the sun is shining over the lake
The smile will entice me
Until the day of never ending depression
The smile is forgotten
I still sit on this cloudy morning wondering who I am

Progressing into this forgotten man
I stare into the stars
Eyes opened wide
Thoughts flying like the birds that leave the north
Depressurizing the air in my lungs
So that I may breathe a little slower
My heart continues to race towards
The freedom of the plains over the open oceans

Heightened by the tragedies around the world
I ponder the thought of death
Surrounded by no loving ones
Who forget about the heart that beats silently
Opaque scenery surrounds the eyesight
For color cannot be found
I frequent memories of days long gone by
Only to deepen the scars of life's treasured moments

Pushing myself up on fragile legs
I stumble to stand alone
Arms outstretched to the angels in the night
To steady the weakened knees
I shout to the heavens for the thankfulness of God
For allowing my soul to survive
Allowing all smiles to become the sun
Shining over the souls of the forgotten

Rivers of Gold

Can't sleep thinking of what's to come
Such a significant part of me has fallen ill
Please God take me instead of her
I pray on bended knee
Selfishness conquers my fragile mind
While dealing with inevitable truths

Drinking to soothe the mind of all that is devastating
Repressing the thoughts of living without you
Laughing at naughty jokes
To ease the tears that are streaming
Please God take me instead of her
Not worrying of how the consequences would affect her

Talking about the what ifs of the doctor's speech
Knowing my opinion is all that matters
On how we proceed
Feeling I am following the same path, I'm unable to stop
Progressively I do more and more
So dreams are filled with sleep not pain

Believing that tomorrows decisions
Are for the better not the worse
Knowing either way
Only God makes the final decision
I slam myself onto my knees forcing myself
To pray in tears of pain
I pray Dear God
Allow my mother to live
So she sees the rivers of gold and
Not the oceans of heaven

Strangest of Strangers

So many mistakes made in the past
Keep me from thinking ahead
Why did I do this or that?
How can I change who I've become?
So many complications keeping me stuck
In this sand I stand upon
Slowly sinking, I grasp for something solid
To keep me above the earth
So I may breathe

Fighting against the anger that consumes
Every inch of my being
Struggling to gain control of my senses
So I can see the light before me
Knowing I am stronger then my actions
I strive to compose my inner thoughts
I must be the one who beats life's struggles
No matter who I may hurt

A walk is just a walk
But memory lane reminds me of whom I once was
That silly immaturity has me stranded
On the island of constant hurricanes
Winds blowing every home into toothpicks
Rain drowning every dream into tears

As I lay me down to rest
I dream of days when sun shines into my darkness
Like a beacon in the night
It shall guide me towards the shore of solidarity
My past may never be forgotten
But my future will always amaze
Even the strangest of strangers

Want To Dream

My nose nestled in your neck
My hands on your breasts
My chest against your back
My midsection pressed firmly against you
My knees tucked in behind yours

We slept like this for hours almost nightly
My pillows still smell of the sweet perfume I bought you
The sheets are tangled and wrinkled like we left them
What have I done to keep this bed so empty?
What can I do to fill it again if only for a few hours?
I miss your smell, your body pressed against mine
I miss the way you tell me you love me
As you stare into my eyes
I miss holding onto you like I was taking my final breath
I long for the day when I can be myself again
Not wanting to end everything
I long for your touch, your smile
Your laughter and your kisses

I'm dying inside thinking about you with my eyes open
I don't want to be without you
I want to be with you every day and every night
Please, I am begging you to tell me what I have to do
To have your heart forever
I miss us. I miss you. I miss me. I miss everything.
Please tell me what I can do to make you see
This house is not a home without you
Please come home. I need you.
I want you. I'm crying for you.
Please tell me this is all a dream and
You are coming to wake me up
For if I never get to cherish forever with you
Then I don't want to dream of anyone else.

No Longer Say

As I walk through the city, I stare at all the beautiful lights
I listen to all the sounds around me and
It allows me to smile
I think I hear your voice but I know it's not you
I believe I see your smile in every woman I see

To not be able to want you is not what I ever dreamed of
To not be able to see you is not what brought me this far
To not be able to hold you
Is like nothing I ever thought of
To not be able to look into your eyes
Is blinding every thought in my brain

As I continue this walk through the city
I can smell you everywhere
The pecan pies baking, the roses blowing within the wind
The no-baked cookies
And the perfume scent on my clothes
All these smells remind me of yesterday
If only yesterday was today

Now with these new rules and forever goodbyes
I can no longer say the words that made you smile
I can no longer speak the truth of what my heart desires
I am not allowed to make you feel good
Or let you see me staring at you
For I have been told to no longer say
I love you

For The World To See

As the sun glistens off the lake
It leaves a shine upon your smile
As we stare at the ducks swimming off in the distance
I can't help but notice how beautiful you are
Your blonde hair blowing in the soft wind
Your blue eyes shinning in the sun
I feel as if I am sitting on the beach
With God's perfect angel

As I hold you I feel as if I have fallen into perfection
There has never been a time I feel more complete
You are the sparkling sunshine that brings me hope
You are the perfect moonlight
That allows me to long for tomorrow

As you lay in my arms just know
I will always keep you safe
I will protect you from everything wrong in this world
For as long as I breathe
You and I are the perfect communion of hope and faith
For all believers of love
Our love is the shining example for the world to see

With All That I Was and I Am Now

Today's the day you made history
What once was a romantic love story
Is now a puddle of misery
As your tears fell upon your face
They fell onto your lips with a salty taste
Forever I prayed for and never I got
What once I longed for I should have not sought
I wished for so many things to come true
Yet I knew it was never going to be just me and you
The thought of you dancing as sexy as you are
Makes me long for the last time we made love
For I saw stars
Not a day will go by that I don't wish you were here
I will always want to be in your arms
Year after year, tear after tear
I miss you already as I write this tonight
Shall I leave the door unlocked when I turn off the lights?
As the tears fall, Baby, I want you to know
You are my everything
As I end this now please remember how
I held your face in my hands and kissed you
With all that I was and I am now

When I Close My Eyes

When I am dreaming I can have everything that I want
I can have all the beautiful women in my arms
Smiling into my eyes
Telling me they love me and want to have my babies
Sleeping is an escape from the reality of misery

Some say when I am sleeping I toss and turn a lot
Some say in the winter I can keep them warm
Even without heat
Some have said I never let them go and hold them
As tight as I can
I must be holding onto the one true love
That escapes my grasp

I think about closing my eyes all day long
And about how my dreams will allow me to smile
Who will it be tonight and will she really love me
Will she allow me to be her everything
Will tonight be the night I finally see
My sunshine and moonlight all in one

As I close my eyes
I am seeing your beautiful smile and wet lips
As I close my eyes
I can feel you holding my head to your heart
As I close my eyes
I can feel the love you have for me with meaning
As I close my eyes
I know with you I can never feel not wanted
So tonight when I close my eyes
The angel that betrays me will be gone forever
In her place will be
The angel that will hold me and allow me
To feel as special

Reflect

Forever is nothing but the future
As the days go by
The history you make will either haunt you or praise you
Live for tomorrow, for today will become just a memory
Tomorrow is the future
And the sun will be shining upon you always

Today is the day we live for
As the minutes tick by towards midnight
We wonder how the day will end
Either you will be wishing for it to continue
Or glad it is finally over
Today was just another day in your life
Tomorrows are closer than you think

Life is what we make it
If we treat people badly, we will live a horrible, lonely life
If we treat people with kindness and love
We will be surrounded by those that love us
Your life is either lonely or very busy
Answering to others who say they need you

Tonight, live your life the way you want it
Have the greatest intentions
To make wonderful, smiling memories
If it turns out to be sad, there's always tomorrow
As it ends
Reflect on what you could have done to make it better

I Am Not Afraid

I am not afraid to say I love you
I am not afraid to show I care
I am not afraid to cry in front of you
I am not afraid to lie on your tummy
I am not afraid to show my emotions
I am not afraid to die for you
I am not afraid to hold your hand in public
I am not afraid of what others may think of us
I am not afraid to miss a day of work to be with you
I am not afraid to stare into your eyes
I am not afraid to commit to forever
I am not afraid to give you children
I am not afraid of what you may say to me
I am not afraid of your angry moods
I am not afraid of your morning breath
I am not afraid of making your dreams come true
I am not afraid of forgiving you
For what you might have done
I am not afraid to beg on knees for you to stay
I am very afraid of you never saying yes
I am very afraid of life without you

Forgotten

Like a whisper unheard in the passing wind
Or the leaf blowing in the dead of night
Such a subtle touch you never felt
Or the glancing look you never saw
The forgotten smile of those you've passed
Or the soft-spoken hello you never heard
The dreams you've had you can't remember
The endless nights you spend so all alone
The tears you've cried only you could feel
The shakes you've had for no reason at all
Like the emptiness in your heart that leaves you lonely
Like the flower on your table that wilts in the sun
I have always been here but yet you never notice
I have spoken softly afraid to startle you
I have dreamt of you at night for only you could see me
I have always been here
But yet your eyes are closed to your surroundings
Open your eyes as I open mine
Let your smile be shown as I show you mine
Let not our love be forgotten
Or hidden under sheets in the closet
But allow it to flourish like the flower
That spreads its petals for the world to admire
Here I am as I have been since the day we crossed paths
Here I am as I shall always be
Not walking away but walking towards you
Don't close your eyes when here I am
Let the world notice
That we are no longer alone and forgotten

I Only Smile When I'm Sleeping

Dreaming saves my heart from aching
Laughter and love fills my memories as if they were real
Rushing to sleep to bring back smiles
No sadness while dreaming of those who've gone

Relaxed under cool sheets I feel the wind
It blows me from memory to memory
Of yesterdays long gone
Escaping the reality of pain and loneliness
If I could just stay in dreams, life would be so much fun

Typing letters never answered
Is not dreaming but being awake
Like being forgotten by those around me
Who never noticed I'm standing up
Tonight I will lay myself back into my comfort space
Where dreams come easily
I will drift into my reality
Where I only smile when I'm sleeping

Darkness

Lost and lonely searching for the road
That evades my eyes
Surrounded by tress and dark places
With no sign of the sky
Feeling as if my world has become one with myself
When shall I finally find the road
That is hidden from my vision?

Thorns deepen into my skin with every step I take
Blood seeming to never stop flowing
Along this river of misery
For every step in this forest
Is like walking in a cave without lights
How shall I ever escape the misery of the darkness?

As I continue to walk towards
Where I believe is my sunlight
I recognize my faults and the mistakes I made
It is I that has allowed myself to be lost in this forest
How shall I ever escape
This never-ending darkness that keeps me blind

Believing in tomorrow
Is like believing in today or right now
I shall overcome this darkness
Even if it means lying in the arms of God
I will always try for the better tomorrow
Even if it means I have to crawl to the light
This darkness may be heavy on the heart
But it's my push to keep me alive and walking

Desolate Soul

Sitting in this empty space
Surrounded by the stars so far above
Thinking of the days passed by
With little to no connections
Favored by none
Connected to the dust that sweeps by in the wind
Considered to be gone
Without the chance to reform my image

Staring like an owl stares into the darkness of night
Searching for something
To allow the smile inside to be seen
Praying to the heavens to notice my existence
Crying behind the eyes of blue
Begging to be noticed by passersby

Secure in my emotions to move in the direction of love
Sacrificing even the littlest of habits that turn those away
Forgiving my soul for believing in future romance
Lazily I lay in the grass staring into
The darkness of emptiness

As I long to be loved and to be held,
Just to be alive in someone else's dreams
I think of the consequences
Of giving up the security of loneliness
The possibilities of never regaining
The peace and serenity I feel now
It'd be so worth the love that could cure t
This desolate soul

Finally Smile

Anger spews inside this heart as I fight to find answers
What once was a blossoming life with family and finances
Has turned into hell
In a struggling ball of yarn rolling uphill
Only captured by those who suffer the same iron fist
That punches us when we smile

No sense of reality
When you can't find the sense of normality
No glorious sunshine
Warming the heart when ice surrounds your every step
Sensual souls grasping at the straws
Thrown out to the poor

Fluttering butterflies
Redeeming Gods creations of beauty and clarity
Watching as they fly away freely
Unstressed by human beings
I wish to be that wonder
So my days can be soon filled with nectar
If by some chance the sunshine is brighter tomorrow
Then maybe once I can finally smile

With Salty Tears

We sit alone in a bed we once made love in
We talk about the past and what went wrong
You lie there crying wanting me to hold you
How did we ever get this far? This is not us
I listen to your words between your sobs
I feel you shake as you can't help yourself
You're telling me everything
That's causing these tears to fall
Where were all these tears hiding? All this pain?
You were an angel
Who flew into my heart and kept it safe
You were an angel
who wrapped me into her arms of love
Now you're an angel so lost you can't see what you had
As you cry I remember why we're losing everything
This bed was shared with another man
The sheets dirtied by the juices of lust
The lies of a heartless wife
Whose love there never really was
For once it is not I that am crying but you
For once I feel I can go on and be me
So as I watch you cry, I know that the pain you feel is real
I know that you are hurting like you hurt me
Fly to the man you chose
The man who makes you happy
The man you hid from me
Go to him and be faithful.
Be his angel.
Be everything I deserved and never got
Be who you want to be
That is his angel
With love so pure for one human being
Good-bye my sweet angel

Good-bye for now and forever
Don't cry
For if you're truly happy you would be smiling
It was you and I against the world
And you promised me forever more
You let me go and the struggle has ended
It's time for me to let you go
Here's the hug you asked for
Here's me kissing away your tears
With salty tears upon my lips
I say I love you
This is your last kiss.
This is our last goodbye.
This is our final fight for love

Shall Always Be Love

Brown eyes gleaming like diamonds on wedding rings
Black hair lying on shoulders like paint on walls
Hands moving rapidly as you speak of your excitement
Possibilities of your night ahead
Speak of pure joy and happiness

The laughter far exceeds any thought of depression
The sincerity of your words lunge into open space
All that hear everything you speak of smile, if even inside
Your happiness drives those around you
To strive to keep up

To think of the new or the beginning of love
Reminds me of yesterday
When the butterflies swarmed
Like monarchs heading south
Consuming my every thought of the one that I loved
Longing to be in her arms
Kissing her gently
Not letting go

To see your happiness
Is what I hope to see in my daughters' eyes
To know they're loved like the water
Flowing through the rainbows
With the understanding that their future
Is filled with family
Allows me to understand
That the greatest feeling
Shall always be love

www.ingramcontent.com/pod-product-compliance
Lightning Source LLC
Chambersburg PA
CBHW071942020426
42331CB00010B/2985